my Favourite Book

Celebrities' Childhood Choice

Compiled by William Watt

Acknowledgements

I would like to thank all the celebrities who contributed to this book. I would also like to thank Libraries and Archives Publications, Pamela McClean, Margaret Thomson, graphic designer, Moira Thorburn, photographer and Heather Thomas, Head of Lending Services for their help and expertise.

Special thanks to Yorkhill Sick Children's Hospital for their co-operation and to DC Thomson Ltd. for allowing the reproduction of the 'Black Bob' illustration.

Every effort has been made to secure permission to include material in this book. The publisher apologises for any errors or omissions and would be grateful to be notified of any corrections.

W Watt

ISBN 0-906169-49-6
Published by Glasgow City Libraries and Archives 1997

Printed By Dorset Printers (GLW) LTD

Glasgow

Introduction

In February 1996 Glasgow City Libraries decided to embark on a new initiative to introduce children to the joy and excitement of books. In these days of television, videos and computer games it is becoming increasingly difficult to get children into the reading habit. In an attempt to reverse this trend we decided to produce a booklist for children containing those titles and authors which well known personalities read and enjoyed when they were children.

We received an overwhelming response to our request for contributions and were delighted at the wide variety of children's titles nominated.

At this point in the project it was decided to invite contributions from a cross-section of Glasgow schoolchildren. Their choices proved as varied and interesting as those chosen by the celebrities.

As this book is for and about children it seemed appropriate to donate all proceeds to Yorkhill Scanner Appeal.

William Watt
Children's Services Librarian

By purchasing this book you will be helping to raise money for Yorkhill Scanner Appeal which has been launched by the Yorkhill Sick Children's Fund. It is proposed to raise £1,500,000 to purchase a Magnetic Resonance Imaging Scanner for the Royal Hospital for Sick Children, Yorkhill. M.R.I. has many advantages over conventional X-Rays and is really the state-of-the-art in diagnostic imaging. Up to 2,000 children a year could benefit from this equipment.

Laurence Anholt
The Catcher in the Rye

Laurence is one of the most versatile authors writing for children today, having written over 40 books.

His choice of titles emphasises the sheer fun of reading and of letting your imagination soar.

“Once I could read, I read everything in sight. From ‘The Cat In The Hat’ to my Dad’s ‘Readers’ Digest’ magazines. I read ‘The Beano’, the back of cereal packets and even detergent bottle labels – Domestos was a particular favourite! Later I moved on to ‘The Catcher In The Rye’, which I loved, and ‘Lord of the Flies’.

But throughout my childhood, my brothers and I were ‘Tintin’ mad. I was a hopeless Hergé addict. We could drive everyone crazy by quoting whole sections from any of those exciting, surreal and funny books.

One night, when I was about 7, my mother crept into my bedroom. As she gently stroked my sleeping head, she was horrified by a strange growth. Was it a hideous boil on the top of my head? No, my mum had discovered my secret plan to grow a Tintin topknot using one of her curlers... “Billions of blue blistering barnacles!” ”

Paddy Ashdown
Kim

As leader of the Liberal Democrats, Paddy is already gearing up his party for what will be one of the most closely fought general elections of recent years. The title which Paddy has chosen shows us that books can have something relevant to say about events in our own lives.

“My favourite was a book entitled ‘Kim’ by Rudyard Kipling.

It tells the story of a boy, named Kim, who was of mixed Indian/English origin. As a young boy, he becomes involved in a series of adventures that involve him with Indian holy men and engage him in spying for the British in the North West Frontier. Like Kim, I too felt uprooted from my friends and familiar surroundings, having just left India for Ireland. I missed India and my friends terribly. But Kipling's eloquent description of India reminded me of the country and people that I knew. Kim's own adventures in the book, served as a reminder of my past in India and that of my family. ”

Cheryl Baker
Heidi Grows Up

Cheryl is well known for her television appearances on television's 'Razzamatazz' and 'Record Breakers'.

Cheryl's choice of book is unusual because it is a sequel to a more famous children's book 'Heidi'.

"The book that made an impact on me when I was a child was 'Heidi Grows Up'. It was my favourite book when I was about 10 years old.

I lived in a block of flats in the East End of London and longed to open my front door on to grass instead of a balcony! 'Heidi Grows Up' was a great escape for me.

I have always enjoyed reading and still read a lot, especially now to my twin daughters, Kyla and Natalie."

Tony Blair
Kidnapped

As a Scotsman, it is fitting that Tony has chosen one of the most exciting Scottish stories ever written.

“When I was a child my favourite book was ‘Kidnapped’ by Robert Louis Stevenson. I enjoyed adventure stories and found this particular one especially well written and exciting.”

Melvyn Bragg
Kidnapped

Best known as presenter of the arts programme 'The South Bank Show' Melvyn is an enthusiastic advocate of books and reading, and has written several highly acclaimed novels.

Melvyn has chosen two excellent books, one of which is a Scottish classic.

"My favourite book from my early childhood, that is to say before the age of 7, was a novel about Robin Hood. Alas, I cannot remember the author but I read and reread it dozens of times.

I do remember reading 'Kidnapped' by R.L. Stevenson, again, when I was quite young. I remember being totally taken up in the thrills and the excitement of the plot and racing to finish it because I wanted the hero's misfortunes to be over. I loved the characters and the strangeness of the way the grown ups behaved as well as the adventures and the descriptions of frightening and desolate places."

Andy Cameron
Treasure Island

Andy is one of Scotland's funniest and most popular comedians who has also proved himself an excellent straight actor, whose choice of book is a true 'Scottish' novel which has never been out of print since it was first published in 1883. This is not a book for one generation, this is a book for all generations.

"My favourite book during my formative years was 'Treasure Island' by Robert Louis Stevenson. The most memorable thing about the book was how I tried to identify with Jim Hawkins and for a period of time every school teacher who gave me a hard time was Long John Silver – even the female teachers!

Recently I've made my two boys read this most excellent book and although they did it under protest they both now are into a 'Tale of Two Cities' which I discovered in an old BB box in the attic. While these books don't quite come up to the level of 'Shoot' magazine in their eyes, I am sure I've helped to whet their appetite for some real adventure in a literary sense and who knows perhaps they'll pick up 'War and Peace' next!"

John Christopher
The Swiss Family Robinson

John's best known work is the 'Tripod Trilogy' consisting of the following titles: 'The White Mountains', 'The City of Gold and Lead' and 'The Pool of Fire'.

The books describe how the Earth is invaded, and mankind enslaved by aliens from space. Some humans refuse to accept their fate and decide to fight back. Their desperate attempts to regain their planet and their freedom make a thrilling read.

If children's literature is capable of this, it is capable of anything. A truly magnificent achievement!

“I propose to cheat by naming two books. The first, 'Swiss Family Robinson', was read to me by my mother at bedtime (before I could read for myself). The second is 'Coral Island'. It was not until well into my middle years that I realised these books heralded the passion which devoured my adolescent years, and whose lingering influence was to dominate a major part of my writing.

In both books the adventure element was, for me anyway, totally subordinate to the main point of identification, which was with people (preferably close to my own age) exploring exotic but strictly plausible new worlds, in contrast with the essential implausibility of fairy tales. In science-fiction of the early thirties this was transferred to the notion of exploring other planets of our solar system. We knew enough about those planets to stimulate the imagination, but lacked the later detailed information which ruled out the possibility of exotic life forms, and left us once again alone in the universe. The possibility of life existing elsewhere in the galaxy remained but our best understanding of science told us that, presuming it did exist, we would never be in a position to make realistic contact. Science-fiction turned into a kind of fairy tale, and I could no longer read it. I wrote books which were put into that category, but I never liked the label. My own speculations were almost entirely earth-bound.

Actually there was a third book. Although an only child and male, I spent my happiest times in the house of my godmother, who had four girls. I used to sit in the boot cupboard and devour old copies of 'Schoolgirl's Weekly'. And I also read, and re-read, the entire Louisa M. Alcott canon. 'Little Women', as I now understand, was concerned with something far more important than the exploration of fantastic landscapes: it was about the exploration of human relationships, an altogether higher subject. I went on subsequently to read Jane Austen, and still do. Alas, I never got within light years of writing like her. ”

Tom Conti
The Famous Five

One of Scotland's finest actors, Tom has won many awards for his theatre and film work and is possibly best known for his role in the award winning film 'Shirley Valentine'.

"My favourite books were 'The Famous Five' and 'Adventure' books of Enid Blyton. They were always exciting; about danger and courage – what children like best from the safety of their own beds."

Ivor Cutler
Andrew Lang's fairy tale collections

Author and poet Ivor Cutler is a very funny man, whose zany, off the wall style of humour is a cross between Spike Milligan and Robin Williams.

"Up until I was 13, I read Andrew Lang's fairy tale collections with enormous satisfaction. I suppose I found the real world too brutal to cope with.

As an adult (from 17) my political and social behaviour have been idealistic, but I doubt if fairy tales have played much of a part. When I became a father I refused to have a television in the house. Books are my drug. I can't get moving for piles of books on the floor."

Alan Douglas
Noddy

Best known as a presenter of BBC's Scottish news programme 'Reporting Scotland', Alan's choice of books reflect his interests as he grew up. Read on and all will be revealed.

“I must confess it is difficult to remember exactly what I read as a child, as it was such a long time ago! However, three books or series occur to me from the depths of my memory. They were:

'Noddy' by Enid Blyton, which probably explains my continuing interest in cars, although slightly faster and more sleek than Noddy's!

A whole collection of 'Rupert the Bear' books, with all sorts of memories of mysterious goings-on with strange professors in obscure laboratories.

Some of the 'Famous Five' books and their graphic adventures, all accompanied by "lashings of ginger beer".”

Blythe Duff
I am David

One of Scotland's finest actresses, Blythe plays the part of Detective Constable Jackie Reid in Scottish Television's award winning series 'Taggart'. With the death of Mark McManus as Detective Chief Inspector Jim Taggart the future of the programme was in doubt. However Blythe and James McPherson, as Detective Sergeant Mike Jardine, have proved more than capable of carrying the show.

" I wish your list had been around when I was young, it might have encouraged me to read more. It's something I don't do enough of. At the moment I'm trying to read more short stories, to kick start my reading. However my school memory was a book called 'I am David' by Anne Holm about a young Jewish boy. When I was in primary 'Pippi Longstocking' by Astrid Lindgren rings a bell. "

Jim Farry
The Famous Five

As Chief Executive of the Scottish Football Association Jim is the guy who gets blamed for most of Scottish football's problems.

It says a lot for Jim's character that he ignores the criticisms and gets on with what is a very difficult job.

"I must confess that I thoroughly enjoyed my visits to the library as a youngster. I was eager to read and therefore 'borrowed' my brother's library ticket to obtain more books. With the passage of time, it is difficult to fully recollect the 'favourite' book although I well remember reading books about 'The Famous Five' and other such adventures. My memory conjures up phrases like "Let's go on a picnic and have lashings of cooling lemonade".

Such are childhood memories of innocent meanderings through the library shelves.

Adventures, travel and excitement are my memories from visits to the library, a world so far removed from my day to day existence. A library ticket was my passport to other lands and ideas! "

Alex Ferguson
Treasure Island

Only the late great Jock Stein could rival Alex's claim as the greatest football manager Scotland has ever produced. The book which Alex has chosen shows that our everyday surroundings can spur us on to read books which fire our imaginations.

"As a young boy growing up by the docks in Glasgow seeing the large ships, I used to think about the book 'Treasure Island', which was a wonderful story. 'Treasure Island' offered excitement and adventure and was definitely one of my favourites."

Donald R. Findlay
Kidnapped

Donald is probably the best known lawyer in Scotland, and has been involved in most of the major court cases in Scotland over the last few years. When not fighting his corner in court, Donald can be found supporting his favourite football team Rangers.

Donald's choice is a truly stirring and exciting tale of mystery, treachery and adventure and he captures the spirit of the book in his comments.

"As a child my favourite book was 'Kidnapped' by Robert Louis Stevenson. I must have read it three or four times when I was young and still read it from time to time now that I am just a little older.

The book always excited me with its tale of the adventures of a young man who seems at times to have the whole world against him and yet constantly manages to succeed despite going from one disaster to another. It is also the classic story of the good guys and the bad guys with a series of wonderful characters with the wicked uncle reminding me of an old man who lived down the road from my home and who had long white hair and a beard and used to frighten the life out of me with his deep booming voice. Most of all the story was set in Scotland and I could actually picture myself as David Balfour, sword in hand, roaming around the Highlands defeating my enemies.

Come to think of it, I might just read it again."

Anne Fine
William's Crowded Hours

Anne has written over 20 books for children, all on different themes but all full of hilarious situations and events. Her best known title is probably 'Madame Doubtfire' which was made into a very funny film starring Robin Williams. The film was excellent, but the book is better.

Anne won the Carnegie Medal for the best children's book published in 1993. 'The Flour Babies'.

“My favourite book was 'William's Crowded Hours' by Richmal Crompton. I loved all the 'William' books all through my childhood. I read them over and over, till the lives and adventures of William and his gang, The Outlaws, and all their friends and enemies were as real to me, or even more real, than my own boring life. I still think they are among the very best books for children ever written (possibly because they began as stories for adults, so there's no element of childishness about them – I hate childish books with a passion). They're brilliantly constructed, and the vocabulary is as rich as anything you'll find in the literature. Have a go!”

Gregor Fisher
Black Bob

Gregor's portrayal of the most famous layabout in Glasgow, Rab C. Nesbitt, has tickled the funny bone of the nation, and has made Rab a cult figure in Scotland.

Gregor has chosen a title I remember well. Black Bob was a Collie sheepdog who was forever getting involved with crooks, sheep stealers and smugglers. Fortunately, Bob was cleverer than all of them and he and his master Andrew Glen still roam their beloved hills.

“I would say when I was very young I enjoyed the book 'Black Bob' which is equivalent to a modern day 'Lassie'.

I believe that this book with many others about animals give children a certain amount of responsibility towards animals.”

Keith Floyd
Swallows and Amazons

Keith is probably the best known of all the TV celebrity chefs. His unstuffy and humorous approach to food and cooking have made him a favourite of the British public.

Keith's choice of book shows how our childhood reading can influence our adult lives.

“When I was about 12 years old, the books that absolutely enthralled me were Arthur Ransome's ‘Swallows and Amazons’, ‘Swallowdale’ and the rest of the related books.

These books gave me terrific enthusiasm for an outdoor life of camping, fishing, sailing and cooking over wood fires. In fact I think they are so good, at the age of 50 I bought all the titles again in paperback for my own daughter to read.”

Dawn French
The Hobbit

As one half of the super comedy duo French and Saunders, Dawn French can lay claim to be one of the funniest comedians on television.

“My favourite book as a child was ‘The Hobbit’ by J.R.R. Tolkien. My father read it to us initially and then, when I was old enough, I read it myself and went on to read the ‘Lord of the Rings’ afterwards. These books and their magic have never left me.”

Rikki Fulton
The Heroes

Rikki is undoubtedly one of the most talented and versatile actors Scotland has ever produced. His comic creations range from the gloomy Rev. I.M. Jolly to the incompetent motor cycle policeman Supercop. Perhaps his most popular character is Francie, one half of Glasgow's most loveable rogues 'Francie and Josie'. Rikki is also highly regarded as a writer and director, and also as a very fine dramatic actor.

"I was very lucky that my mother and father gave me the most wonderful Christmas present one year, when I was even younger than you are now. It was a set of eight beautiful, cloth-bound books, which, naturally, became my all-time favourites, and gave me a life-long love of books as things of beauty as well as providing the joy of reading.

I can remember the titles, and even the colours to this day, 'Treasure Island' by Robert Louis Stevenson, 'Grimm's Fairy Tales', 'The Tales of Hans Christian Andersen'; 'Alice in Wonderland' and 'Alice Through the Looking Glass' by Lewis Carroll, 'Gulliver's Travels' by Jonathan Swift, 'Swiss Family Robinson' by J.R. Weiss; 'Arabian Nights' by Almost Everybody and 'The Heroes' (my number one favourite) by Charles Kingsley. I am still an avid reader as is my wife Kate, but nowadays I enjoy crime fiction by the more respected authors like P.D. James and Ruth Rendell. I hope that you will continue to read and enjoy all kinds of books."

Gareth Hale
Under Milk Wood

As one half of the comedy team Hale and Pace, Gareth has been responsible for some of the funniest and most original comedy on television today.

One of Gareth's choices is a fascinating one in that it is not a novel, but a play. Dylan Thomas wrote the play 'Under Milk Wood' for radio and he described it as "a play for voices", and what magnificent voices they are!

"I'm afraid I'm going to have to cheat, and choose two books. When I was at Junior level J. Meade Falkner's 'Moonfleet' provided mystery, tension and excitement in a perfect combination, guaranteed to scare the pants off any youngster.

At secondary school I was introduced to the works of Dylan Thomas and became very close friends, literally. My favourite work is 'Under Milk Wood'. His creation of characters, use of dialogue and injection of comedy drew me instantly, and like so many of the greats he makes it accessible. It's written for everybody, not just a select few."

Cliff Hanley
The 'Greyfriars' titles

Journalist, author, broadcaster, songwriter (Cliff wrote the words to 'Scotland the Brave'), Cliff Hanley is a man of many parts. Cliff is a well known face around Glasgow and his knowledge of his native city is encyclopaedic.

Cliff lists as his favourite books the 'Greyfriars' titles written by Frank Richards. Greyfriars school's most famous pupil was undoubtedly Billy Bunter. Sneaky, lazy, greedy, cowardly, Bunter was all these things and more. Many of the 'Billy Bunter' books have been updated to appeal to children of today. They are very funny books with tremendous characters. Ask the library staff to order you a Bunter book, you won't regret it.

" In boyhood I was an anglicised wee snob. Classmates read the 'Rover' and the 'Wizard'. I read the 'Magnet', which consisted mainly of life at Greyfriars School, very upper-class. It starred Harry Wharton and the Famous Five; and comic relief was supplied by the fatty Billy Bunter, who was really thick and therefore my favourite character.

These tales were written by Frank Richards.

The fascination was that the tales were legends from another planet. I actually enjoyed school because I was a smart alec and won prizes. I wouldn't really have enjoyed Greyfriars because it had no girls. But Richards also had stories in the 'Girls Own Paper', in which you would find sisters and cousins of the Greyfriars boys. I gobbled all the tales. They were real life, while my own daily drag was a dim fantasy. It was only later that I discovered that fantasy is what life is about. "

Mairi Hedderwick
The Island of Adventure

Mairi Hedderwick's beautifully illustrated books depict the rugged beauty of Scottish island life. Probably best known to children for her books describing the adventures of the resourceful Katie Morag on the Island of Struay. Mairi has also written books for adults and illustrated books written by other authors.

"I'm afraid I will possibly let you down, politically correctly, that is, as I shamefully admit to Enid Blyton's 'Adventure' series as my abiding passion as a child.

The books usually came out in the summer holidays. One particular summer I remember waiting outside the local newsagent and book shop in Gourock, early morning, till it had opened, clutching hot holiday money in my hand. 'The Island of Adventure' was soon to be mine and I could not wait to get home – a very long uphill walk – to get started.

That was the book along with 'The Sea of Adventure' that definitely, passionately, headed me at an early age in the direction of where I finally chose to live as an adult. In 'The Sea of Adventure' I read the word Hebrides for the first time. The feeling of tingling excitement at that name is still with me.

'The Mountain of Adventure', 'The Valley of Adventure', 'The Castle of Adventure', and whatever other titles in the series never quite had the same impact. It was sea and islands that held a magical appeal. The excitement of the journey in a boat (a kind of moving island) to an island destination where the sea could dictate whether you could land – or leave. The thought of being stranded on the island (unbelievable to some) safe, secure, thrilling. I still feel that many years on. I love a wild winter storm ...

Enid Blyton's other series bored me. 'The Secret Seven', tho' adventurous, never gave me a location, a sense of place that I could identify with, want to find for myself. That was the primary ingredient for me in the adventure stories. My favourite reading as an adult is travel books.

Enid Blyton definitely sowed the seeds of travel and exploration in me.

My childhood reading material, (in a home that did not have any children's books as we know them today) before the discovery of the 'Adventure' series, consisted of the Bible and very boring school books. But I found 'Pilgrim's Progress' beside the Bible and loved it. Another journey! – tho' mightily weighted down with trials and tribulations. But imagine the delights of the 'Sea of Adventure' compared to poor Pilgrim's Slough of Despond!

A whole new easy-to-read-about-world had opened out. ”

Jane Horrocks
The Lion, the Witch and the Wardrobe

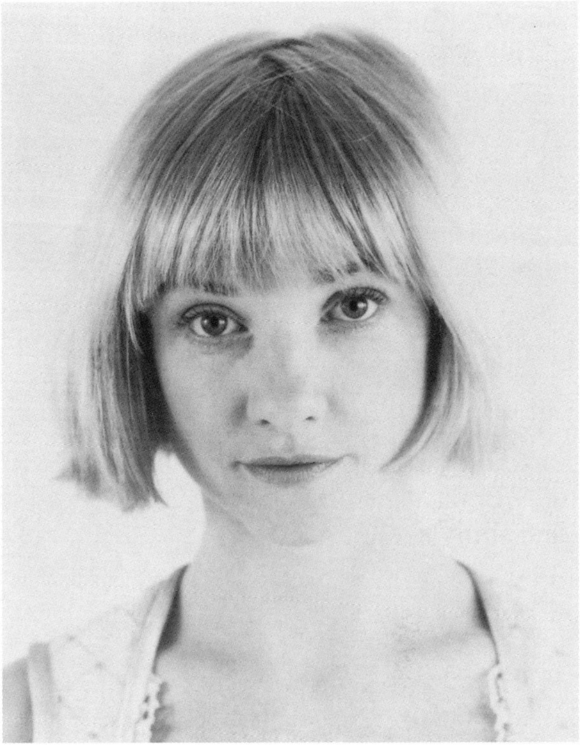

Jane played Jennifer Saunders wonderfully dippy secretary Bubbles in the comedy series 'Absolutely Fabulous'.

Her choice illustrates the role that regular storytimes play in shaping our future reading habits.

“My favourite book as a child was 'The Lion, the Witch and the Wardrobe' by C.S. Lewis. My nan used to read it to me and my brothers and cousins as children.

It was a marvellous book for just before bedtime. The imagination ran riot, and I **still** carry vivid images of this book in my head.”

Lorraine Kelly
Just So Stories

Lorraine is best known as one of the presenters of GMTV where her bubbly and down to earth manner is just what is required first thing in the morning.

The move from local journalist to big time television presenter has proved easy for Lorraine, and I am sure that she will be on our television screens for a long time to come.

“My favourite books were:

All the 'Just Williams', the 'St. Clare' and 'Mallory Towers' series by Enid Blyton.

'Just So Stories' by Rudyard Kipling was probably the one I loved best.

My mum taught me to read before I went to school and I have discovered a world of magic in books. I devour books – and have done since the age of 4+.

I cannot imagine what life would be like if I didn't have the opportunity to curl up with a good book and of course, I have it all to come again with my daughter Rosie. I am so looking forward to rediscovering all my old favourites with her.”

Sir Ludovic Kennedy
The Child's Garden of Verses

Born in Edinburgh, Ludovic is one of Britain's most respected and admired journalists and broadcasters. Ludovic is well known for several books outlining what he considers to be miscarriages of justice.

As his favourite title Ludovic has chosen 'The Child's Garden of Verses' by Robert Louis Stevenson. Stevenson was often ill and many of the poems in the book were written while he was in bed suffering from tuberculosis. He made an attempt in the poems to re-create the emotions and sensations of his own childhood. It is a charming book.

"At the cost of mentioning the name of a book, which I imagine many Scots men and women will be recommending to you, I would unhesitatingly say 'The Child's Garden of Verses' by Robert Louis Stevenson. I adored having these poems read to me and I identified with Leerie, the lamplighter, who posted down my grandfather's house in Belgrave Crescent in Edinburgh. I also identified with the poem about putting boats into the water of Leith, with my doing the same thing a few miles further downstream from RLS, as it flowed by the Belgrave Crescent Gardens. And it was the same with all the other poems in that delightful book. Scots children visiting Edinburgh today, or living in the town, could also benefit, I feel sure.

I would like to recommend one particular poem, 'The Boy in the Train' by M.C. Smith, it has long been a favourite of my wife and myself. ”

Whit wey does the engine say Toot-toot?
Is it feart to gang in the tunnel
Whit wey is the furnace no pit oot
When the rain gangs doon the funnel?
What'll I hae for my tea the nicht?
A herrin', or maybe a haddie?
Has Gran'ma gotten electric licht?
Is the next stop Kirkcaddy?

There's a hoodie-craw on yon turnip-raw!
An' sea-gulls! – sax or seeven.
I'll no fa'oot o' the windae, Maw,
It's sneckit, as sure as I'm leevin'.
We're into the tunnell!, we're a' in the dark!
But dinna be frichtit, Daddy,
We'll sune be comin' to Beveridge Park.
And the next stop's Kirkcaddy!

Is yon the mune I see in the sky?
It's awfu' wee an' curly.
See! there's a coo and a cauf ootbye,
An' a lassie pu'in' a hurly!
He's chackit the tickets and gien them back.
Sae gie me my ain yin, Daddy.
Lift doon the bag frae the luggage rack,
For the next's stop's Kirkcaddy!

There's a gey wheen boats at the harbour mou'
And eh! dae ye see the cruisers?
The cinamon drop I was sookin' the noo
Has tummelt an' stuckt tae ma troosers...
I'll sune be ringin' ma Gran'ma's bell,
She'll cry, "Come ben, ma laddie,"
For I ken mysel' by the queer-like smell
That the next stop's Kirkcaddy!

Dick King-Smith
Tarka the Otter

The recent success of the film 'Babe' based on his book 'The Sheep Pig' has encouraged even more children to seek out the stories of Dick King-Smith, and what wonderful and funny stories they are!

" Not surprisingly perhaps, Dick has chosen as his favourite children's book, one of the most famous and exciting animal stories ever written.

'Tarka The Otter' by Henry Williamson is perhaps one of the greatest of all animal stories, as easily readable by adults as by children.

It contains wonderfully accurate and evocative descriptions of the natural world in general and of otters in particular, and it deals with the cruelties of life as with its joys.

My old edition has splendid woodcut illustrations (by C.F. Tunnicliffe I think) which enhance this most skilful and moving of tales. I loved it as a child and I love it still. "

Lord Provost – Pat Lally
Just William

Pat is the first Lord Provost of the new Glasgow City Council, whose connection with local politics goes back to 1966. He has been instrumental in many of the major improvements in Glasgow over the years.

“As a child my favourite books were the 'Just William' stories. William managed to do things I could only think about, and not actually do for fear of being caught.

I often wondered what exotic food blancmange must be in comparison to my custard.”

Joan Lingard
Just William

As a child, Joan admits to being 'crazy about books'. It was this love of books which led Joan to pick up her pen and write over 20 highly acclaimed books for children. Perhaps Joan's most popular titles are the 5 books which make up the 'Kevin and Sadie' series, about Protestant Sadie who becomes friends with Catholic Kevin in 1970's Belfast. The books are marvellously written, and the issues of religious bigotry and intolerance which they explore, are as relevant today as they were then.

"I am cheating a little and mentioning more than one book, so hope that it is okay. I am not making any quality judgements so I am putting Enid Blyton in with the rest as I enjoyed her books very much at one stage in my life.

It is very difficult for me to pick out just one book from childhood. At each stage in my life my favourite would have been different. Thus, depending on when I would have been asked, I might have chosen Enid Blyton's 'Famous Five', 'Grimm's Fairy Tales', 'Black Beauty' by Anna Sewell, 'Swallows and Amazons' by Arthur Ransome, 'The Chalet School' by Elinor M. Brent-Dyer, 'Biggles' by Captain Johns, 'The Wind in the Willows' by Kenneth Grahame. I was an avid reader. I read everything in my local library at least once. And I read every book I owned over and over again. I felt as if I were sharing in the lives of the characters and in this way I expanded my world.

But if I am forced to pick out one book or one collection of books I think it has to be 'William' by Richmal Crompton. I loved the character and humour. He always made me laugh and he still does, which must be a good testimony after all these years! I used to think it would be fun to be around with William, not knowing what pranks he would innocently and in his bumbling way get up to next. It might not have been possible in the flesh but it was in my imagination. He gave me much pleasure. ”

Jimmy Logan
Swiss Family Robinson

Jimmy hasn't actually been around forever, it just seems as if he has. He is one of the busiest people in Scottish theatre, and rather than slowing down as the years pass, Jimmy seems to get busier and busier. There is probably no aspect of theatre and television that he has not been involved in.

Incidentally, Walt Disney made a very successful film of 'Swiss Family Robinson'. Good film, great book! Read it and find out for yourself!

“If I could speak to a child I would say:-

> 'Swiss Family Robinson' is a story of adventure but it involves the complete family not just you, but all the family stranded on a desert island. Imagine this happening to you, if you were part of this family. Wondering if anybody knows where you are and if you will ever be found.

Imagine what you would do if you were stranded on an island without television. No milk in the morning for your cornflakes because there was no milkman and no cornflakes, no paper shop to buy a comic, no frying pan, in fact nothing but what you had to make, adapt or find, to eat, drink or just do to fill in the time.

You would be so busy trying to survive that you would not have time to wonder what to do. How do you light a fire? Yes I know, rub two sticks together but have you ever tried it? I was in the Boy Scouts and I think I only did it once and it took hours. Without a fire you would not survive, so you have to learn to do things like that, whether you like it or not!

Keeping warm, keeping dry and having to hunt for your food. Some people are good at that but on this island you have to do your share... just to live.

In this book you read how an ordinary family who had never been in this situation before have to learn and have to live together whether they like it or not.

Could you do it?

Read how they did and became better people with more understanding of life, living and of how to get on with other people.

It even teaches you how to get on with people you don't like!

Try it. ”

Joanna Lumley
Tom Sawyer

Joanna is probably best known to young people as the ghastly Patsy Stone in the hit comedy series 'Absolutely Fabulous'.

It is interesting that Joanna picks a book which is often regarded as the 'ultimate' adventure book for boys. Joanna is correct of course, there are no such things as boys' books or girls' books, there are only books, to be enjoyed by everyone.

"One of my favourite books was 'Tom Sawyer' by Mark Twain. I was hooked from the whitewashing of the fence onwards and still think that Injun Joe's death was the most gruesome I have ever read. Yippee! I recommend it to all youngsters."

Viv Lumsden
The Famous Five

Viv is well known as a newsreader and presenter of STV's news programme 'Scotland Today' and is married to Alan Douglas.

"I'm afraid I was another Blyton fan – 'The Famous Five' being my favourite. The only other book I remember to make an impact on me is 'The Moonspinners' by Mary Stewart. I read it around the age of 12. It was a beguiling mix of romance and excitement."

Fergus McCann
The Tree in the Trail

When Fergus stepped in to save Celtic Football Club in 1994 he became one of the major players in Scottish football.

His choice of book is an interesting one, and the story itself sounds intriguing.

“My favourite book as a child was ‘The Tree in the Trail’ by Holling Clancy Holling.

This tells how things and people change throughout the lifetime of a Cottonwood Tree.”

Jack McLean
Oliver Twist

Jack is well known for his outspoken and often very funny column in The Herald newspaper, and has spoken out many times of the importance of libraries and reading.

Jack has chosen a title which may surprise adult readers of his column, but children everywhere will recognise the book as a 'true' classic.

"You can't decide on a favourite book anymore than you can pick out the best film you ever saw. It's a bit like 'Desert Island Discs'. I've tried for years to think up my eight records and I would refuse to go on the programme because I would want to take 800 records anyway.

However a while back I was asked what book I would recommend for a ten year old. She was taking part in a competition organised by the Scottish Library Association, and I was glad to write about my favourite books. Mine was 'Oliver Twist' by Charles Dickens which I first read when I was seven, the book was abridged for children, but was still very scary. It was magnificently illustrated by Dudley D.

Watkins, the artist who created the 'Oor Wullie' and 'The Broons' comic strips. The book I ended up recommending for ten year olds however was Frances Hodgson Burnett's classic, 'The Secret Garden'. It is a story for both boys and girls. It is for boys and girls like me who had a wee secret garden for ourselves, one the adults either didn't know about, or kept us in the dark about. It was a fertile garden you could cultivate yourself, you grew fantasies and ideas like plants, you grew as fragrant as flowers.

Books for children are straight out of 'Alice in Wonderland'. Eat me. Drink me. Be bigger. Be smaller. The truth is that Alice wasn't in Wonderland; she was straight out of Dante's parish and there is a darkness in the beginning of the Secret Garden, and then the garden grows and the sun shines. For a start it is a wonderful read and more. It is something which tells you how to have your own world light and sunny as well as dark and grave. Adults still give the book to their nieces. If they have any sense they will give it to their nephews as well. Who knows if children will be reading a hundred years from now. I hope they are. For books are the secret garden. Your own at that, and visitors are by invitation only. ”

Adam McNaughtan
Tough of the Track

Best known perhaps as a folk singer/songwriter, Adam not only has more strings to his bow than anyone else, he has more bows than anyone else! Singer, writer, teacher (retired), bookseller, songwriter, Adam refuses to be pigeon holed.

“My reading in my primary school days was more voracious than selective. I regularly read seven comics a week, not counting my sister's. I suspect that 'Tough of the Track' and 'Lord Snooty' had as much to do with my literary development as Alan Breck and Darsie Latimer.

I was never a great one for reading books over and over, and the fodder I got from Dennistoun Public Library was the usual Frank Richards, Richmal Crompton and Percy F. Westerman. During the summer holidays I would borrow the regulation two books first thing in the morning, read them and go back to borrow two more before the library closed.

At the age of six, however, I was given as a school prize, chosen by my teacher, Lavinia Derwent's 'Adventures of Tammy Troot'. Govey Dick, how I enjoyed it! Obviously the authorities were not too worried about my picking up bad habits of speech or writing from a rat and a fish discussing whether Cuddy-Loup-the-Dyke was the correct name for leap-frog. So at that early age I learned that even animals said 'hame' and 'stane' if they were Scottish.

My reading was, of course, supported by the regular radio broadcasts of the stories on 'Children's Hour' and the dialogue I heard in my mind as I read was always in the tones of W.H.D. Joss. I do not know that the obvious message of Tammy's pride being brought low has made me any less bumptious but I enjoyed the humour in the relationship between fish, rat and fat, wheezy Froggy. ”

Catherine MacPhail
Little Women

Catherine won the Kathleen Fidler award in 1994 for her children's book 'Run Zan Run'. This is a fast paced and thought provoking story of bullying and its consequences. Catherine has written for television and radio with great success. Her next children's novel is eagerly awaited.

"All through primary school I had one favourite book which I read over and over again. It was 'Little Women' by Louisa May Alcott. The story of four sisters and their mother and all the things that happen to them while their father is off at the war. I loved it because it was funny and it was sad, but most of all I loved it because I could relate to it so much. You see, I was one of four sisters too. We lived in a close in Greenock with our mother. Like the March girls, our father was not there. However, our father was dead. Like the March girls we were poor, (although I could never understand how they could be poor and still have a servant!) But I could see so much of the fun that those girls had reflected in the fun my sisters and I had. We used to put on plays just like the March girls. We used to harmonise and on many occasions we just used to fight.

We were always doing things together and my mother loved that. I even tried calling my mother Marmee like the March girls, thinking it sounded so much posher than **mammy**, but my sisters spoiled it by making a fool of me. I tended to be the butt of their jokes because I was always doing something daft. I was the eejit in the family. I first got my love of comedy and Scottish humour from my sisters. They never took anything I said seriously and were always pulling the rug from under my feet whenever I tried to be too serious. There was always a lot of laughter in our family. I wanted to be like all the March girls. A writer like Jo, sensible like Meg, gentle like Beth (although I drew the line at dying young) and pretty like Amy. Jo in the book tries to write adventures but only succeeds when she looks at her own family and writes about them. Little Women made me look and appreciate my own life and to this day it is still one of my favourite books. **”**

John Major
Billy Bunter

I am particularly pleased that the Prime Minister found time to contribute to the book list. He is a very busy man, but he obviously appreciates the importance of reading.

“When I was a child I enjoyed the ‘Billy Bunter’ books by Frank Richards, ‘20,000 Leagues Under the Sea’ by Jules Verne, ‘Below the Salt’ by Thomas Costain as well as ‘The Adventures of Robin Hood’ and ‘King Arthur and his Knights of the Round Table’ both written by Roger Lancelyn Green.”

Andrew Miller
Moonfleet

As Director of Libraries for Glasgow, Andrew is responsible for all of Glasgow's libraries. Andrew's choices are 'classic' children's books in the truest sense. 'Moonfleet' was written in 1898 and 'White Fang' written in 1906, and they have never been out of print in all that time. These 2 books are as thrilling to children of today as they were to children of 90 years ago. Request them free at your library and prepare to be thrilled!

"I am a voracious reader and it does not matter whether it is books or sauce bottle labels. Things have progressed to such a point that I often have to visit museums without my family who become impatient because I read every word on every notice and label.

In my time I must have read and re-read thousands of books. I keep my personal copies of C.S. Forrester's Hornblower series close at hand just in case I ever have nothing to read. Looking back however, two books stand out as 'unput-downable'.

The first was 'Moonfleet' by John Falkner, a story about smugglers, crypts and treasure. It was made into a film which I enjoyed as well, but not as much as I enjoyed the story in my own imagination especially when... no, find out for yourself.

My second recommendation is Jack London's 'White Fang'. It does no justice to say this is a story about a dog or even a fighting dog. It is about a dog conditioned to fight, but the sheer satisfaction I remember even today as in the different events White Fang triumphs must place 'White Fang' into the category of a 'great page turner'.

As a public librarian I have issued library membership to many people over an increasing number of years and envied them the opportunity of meeting and reading my favourite books for the first time. I envy you too, so get reading. ”

Dannii Minogue
Are you there God?
It's me, Margaret

Dannii first appeared on our screens in the Australian television soap 'Home and Away'. Since then she has appeared on 'The Big Breakfast' and has co-hosted many children's programmes. As if that wasn't enough she also found time to have several top ten chart hits.

"A book that had a great impact on me when I was going into my teens was 'Are you There God? It's me, Margaret' by Judy Blume. It's a story of a girl growing up, getting her period, perving on boys and all the other stuff that seems so mysterious at that age. She writes in a natural, funny way, that is like reading someone's thoughts. It's good to know you're not the only one totally confused."

Katy Murphy
Black Beauty

Katy shot to fame playing the role of Miss Toner, the hapless assistant to Eddie Clockerty in the hit TV series Tutti Frutti. She is now a well respected and established actress both on television and in the theatre.

“I support very much any scheme which encourages children to read for pleasure rather than just to pass exams as I think it is a joy not to be missed.

The first book which sprung to mind when I read your letter was 'Black Beauty' by Anna Sewell, so I guess I should stick to that one. This book made a very powerful impression on me eliciting vividly recalled emotional responses. I loved Beauty, Ginger and the rest and cried my eyes out when poor Ginger died through lack of care. I suppose ultimately I found the book involving on every level, and such absorption in a story, an active as opposed to passive absorption, is a very specific pleasure and resulted in a lifelong addiction to books.”

Ian Pattison
The Adventures of Robin Hood

Ian is the creator of that Glasgow scallywag, Rab C. Nesbitt. Ian's humorous slant on the characters of Glasgow have been responsible for many moments of absolute hilarity. 'Atletico Partick' which was recently on television was also written by Ian and was a hilarious study of amateur footballers, very, very amateur footballers.

"My favourite was 'The Adventures of Robin Hood' by Roger Lancelyn Green. I borrowed it from the school library as an eight year old and managed to hold onto it for a full six months before a sense of guilt overcame me and I returned it. I still remember the sense of loss at handing it back and the terrible pang of jealousy at the prospect of someone else borrowing it. Matter of fact I'm getting quite wound up writing this. I think I'll go buy another copy."

Terry Pratchett
The Moomintroll

Terry Pratchett is the creator of that madcap alternative world 'Discworld'. In a series of hilarious books, Terry introduces the reader to a travel trunk with legs, talking demons, bad tempered witches and a tortoise who carries 'Discworld' around on its back.

The Discworld novels are particularly popular with teenagers and young people.

"After a lot of thought I'm going for **two** sets of books:

'The Moomintroll' books by Tove Jansson and the 'Just William' books, by Richmal Crompton.

The 'William' books might seem dated now – the best ones are set around or during the Second World War. But they've survived a lot better than the 'Famous Five' or the 'Secret Seven' or 'Swallows and Amazons', which always seemed to me to be taking place in some unreal world even when I first read them. William is a kid. He hangs out with his friends, although in those days it was called 'hanging around'. And although he always has the best of intentions he always lands in trouble.

The writing is good and not at all patronising, and for me the key delight of the books was the way in which William (who stayed aged eleven for years) managed to annoy the pompous adults who really needed annoying. I wanted to be William when I was eleven. I'd give quite a lot of money to be him now!

I learned a lot from the books – the use of irony, how real humour develops not from jokes, and how a whole character can be described by just one simple line...

'The Moomintroll' are even more out of place in these days when heroes are made of plastic. The series looks as if it is for very young children, and in a way it is – a family of hippo-shaped creatures have adventures in and around a mythical valley in Finland. Doesn't sound too promising, put like that. And then I found that I could still re-read them with pleasure when I was 14 – or now I'm 48, come to that. Tove Jansson is a genius of a writer. The books have what I call 'onion skins'; on the surface these Moomintrolls are jolly little fat creatures, and then as you get older you see all the things you missed, the sad darkness around their sunny little world, the wistful Nordic gloom (try 'Moominland in Midwinter' for this) which is also funny.

Both those series taught me the valuable lesson that real humour isn't simply 'jokes' but develops naturally from situations. ”

Frank Rodgers
Bows Against the Barons

Frank has written over 30 books for children ranging from books on how to draw cartoons to a boy who discovers that his teacher is an alien, to a family who have a time travelling kitchen.

His books are very funny and if you read one you will probably want to read the rest. So why not order some of Frank's books at your local library?

"When I was young I remember playing with my pals at being Robin Hood and his Merry Men. We had great fun running through the woods with our home-made bows and arrows pretending we were outlaws on the run from the dastardly Sheriff of Nottingham and the even more dastardly King John. At the end of our game, like the stories and films we had seen, King Richard the Lionheart came back to join forces with Robin and defeat the terrible twosome. King Richard then pardoned Robin and the outlaws, the peasants rejoiced and went back to their cosy little huts and everyone lived happily ever after.

This version of events, of course, was very like a fairy tale. A glossy legend about good and evil. I enjoyed it like that... it was stirring and uncomplicated. But, of course it wasn't true.

For my ninth birthday my aunt gave me a copy of 'Bows Against The Barons', and as I read it I realised that if Robin Hood had really existed, then this is what his life would have been like. It was still noble and stirring, but this time it felt real. The Robin Hood in this book was a true rebel. A man who fought for his people against the tyranny of the king and the nobles. A man who dreamed of ridding the country of the cruel masters who treated the peasants harshly. Masters who, for instance, would order a man's hand or ear to be cut off if he couldn't pay his taxes. This Robin, I realised, was not the kind of man who would have bowed before the king, but a man who had a conscience about the terrible things that were happening to the poor people all around him.

By the end of the book I think I had grown up a little. I had come to understand a bit about how people of conscience can fight and die for their principles... and how in fact, the Robin Hood story is still being re-enacted all round the world where there is tyranny and oppression. I had identified quite strongly with the main character in the book, a young lad named Dickon, and because of that was able to put myself in his position, feel his anger, his excitement, his happiness and sadness.

This, of course, is the power of books. The magic quality they have that transports you into other worlds, exciting and stimulating you... changing you. 'Bows Against the Barons' gave me the feeling that not only had I learned something important about human nature but also made me realise that I would never look at fairy tales or legends in quite the same way ever again. ”

Tony Roper
Tom Sawyer

Tony is a difficult man to pin down. He is an actor, writer, funnyman, playwright and football fanatic, and played Rab C. Nesbitt's rascal of a pal Jamesie Cotter.

Tony wrote the hugely successful play of bygone Glasgow 'The Steamie'. If 'The Steamie' appears at a theatre near you, beg your parents to take you. Promise to wash the dishes for a week, promise anything, just get them to take you. You will laugh yourself silly!

"I understand the difficulty it must be these days to get youngsters to **read** rather than **watch.** I am now fifty-five and can well remember my astonishment as a youngster, the first time I entered a Public Library, it was in McIntyre Street, Anderston. I was there for hours and the book I eventually selected was Mark Twains 'Tom Sawyer'- and from then on I was an avid reader of all adventure stories; and indeed still am. What captivated me? Escape into another world, another time, another culture, and above all having my imagination activated, stimulated, and consecrated by another human being. Like radio drama a book has always got better scenery than any Hollywood extravaganza – and for me a well told yarn has always easily outdone, fifty corpses, 12 car chases, 100 buckets of blood and the endless cops and villains that spew out of the box in the living room. However the writing was on the wall for genuine young readers when the old comics such as 'Adventure', 'Wizard', 'Hotspur', 'Rover' stopped having a prose format and switched to a picture cartoon form. However, I still have a 1937-38 'Boys Own Annual' and that I can Read till my heart's content."

Carol Smillie
The Lion,the Witch and the Wardrobe

Carol Smillie

Carol is a former Miss Scotland who has made the successful transition from model to television personality.

"My favourite book was 'The Lion the Witch and the Wardrobe' by C.S. Lewis.

I was completely fascinated by the fantasy world of Narnia and always imagined it could really happen to me too!"

Mari Steven
The Palomino Pony Books

Mari Steven
from 'CHARTBITE'

SCOTTISH TELEVISION ENTERPRISES

Mari is the co-presenter of STV's pop show 'Chartbite', her choices remind us that there is a wide variety of books for children, many using illustrations as the main method of telling the story.

"I read a lot of pony club types of books when I was young. 'The Palomino Pony' range of books etc. I also loved 'Tintin' and 'Asterix' for fun. A book that always sticks in my mind is 'The Hill of the Red Fox' by Alan Campbell McLean – it is an adventure book about a boy who gets involved in a mystery on a Scottish island."

Lady Thatcher
A Tale of Two Cities

Margaret Thatcher entered the history books on the 4th May, 1979, when she became Britain's first woman Prime Minister.

"I have read your letter with great interest and I am delighted that Glasgow City Libraries and Archives have launched a new initiative to encourage children to read more.

I read avidly as a child and my favourite book was Charles Dickens' 'A Tale of Two Cities'.

I hope that the children benefit enormously from your efforts."

Rob Wainwright
The Lord of the Rings

As Captain of Scotland's Rugby team, Rob has a tricky job in steering the team through the early days of professionalism in the sport. Rob came within a whisker of leading Scotland to the Grand Slam last year, maybe this year Scotland can go one better.

Rob's choice is 'The Lord of the Rings' by J.R.R. Tolkien, a stirring tale of hobbits and dwarves who fight the magical forces of evil. 'The Lord of the Rings' is actually made up of 3 books. Tolkien wrote another classic book about hobbits, dragons and magic, called 'The Hobbit'. Reading 'The Hobbit' is an excellent introduction into the magical world of Tolkien.

“My favourite childhood book was 'Lord of the Rings' by J.R.R. Tolkien.

This was a fantastic fantasy adventure which really grips the reader. I remember finding Earth particularly boring after my trips to Middle - Earth.”

Terry Waite
Just William

As special envoy to the Archbishop of Canterbury, Terry travelled to Beirut in Lebanon to try and negotiate the release of hostages there who had been kidnapped. While on this worthwhile mission Terry was himself kidnapped on 20th January 1987 and was held in captivity until 18th November 1991, a total of 1,762 days.

“I'm afraid that my childhood taste in reading was rather simple. I lived in a small village without a library and thus had to depend upon second hand rummage sales for my supply of books. I greatly enjoyed 'William' books by Richmal Crompton and I suppose I enjoyed them because William Brown held his own against the adults who figured in his life and also because he got into the most terrible trouble without ever running into total disaster. I'm pleased to see that these books are now enjoying a revival. Books which also caught my attention were 'Romany Series' by the BBC Naturalist G. Bramwell Evens. I fear these have not been reprinted and so perhaps it is little use mentioning them. 'Masterman Ready' by Captain Marryat and 'The Coral Island' by R.M. Ballantyne were typical of the books which enabled me to travel in my imagination across the seven seas, also all the Arthur Ransome books. Alison Uttley charmed me with her simple stories of rural life and 'Tom Brown's Schooldays' opened my eyes to a world that was totally alien to me. Although I don't recommend it, 'Little Lord Fauntleroy' did the same. This was a book I didn't want to keep and I remember offering it to my school library. They refused it!

Books brought me great happiness as a child and they continue to do so.”

Richard Wilson
Andersonville

'One Foot in the Grave' is one of the funniest television programmes of recent years. In grumpy Victor Meldrew, Richard has created a magnificent comedy character, his bewildered facial expressions and plaintive cry of 'I don't believe it' are instantly recognisable.

“My childhood reading was very much run of the mill, the usual stuff, but I remember in my early teens being tremendously impressed when I read 'Andersonville' by MacKinlay Kantor. It managed to combine a great sense of period with a strong narrative thrust. Despite the fact of its many characters they all seemed to stand out quite individually and clearly. It was also one of the first anti-war books I had read.”

Baillie John H. Young
Just William

Baillie Young is the Leader of the Conservative group in Glasgow City Council and as such is a long time political opponent of Provost Pat Lally. How interesting therefore that these 2 well known faces in the Glasgow political arena should choose the same book!

“When I was nearly nine years of age the Second World War broke out and I like many others was evacuated and much of the next five or six years was coloured by the War. This included our reading habits, our heroes of the time, and the various ambitions and aspirations that children have.

I loved all the 'Just William' stories and indeed as a small boy very much identified with Miss Crompton's writings. Even when the TV resurrected the idea of Just William in the last few years I spent some happy times watching same! I also liked authors like G.A. Henty who is probably not even heard of nowadays at schools or anywhere else and earlier than that I certainly liked as a very small child 'Alice in Wonderland', 'Bambi' and indeed any books to do with animals.

I think at twelve or thirteen years of age, two books which made an impact on me were the 'White Company' by Arthur Conan Doyle and the other was Buchan's 'The 39 Steps'. One had a sense of history in it which I have also loved, and the other had a sense of an adventure, I could very much identify with Richard Hannay.

I liked all books and still do but perhaps these memories of childhood stick with me even to this day. I appreciate that perhaps I am not detailing the effects they had on me but nevertheless I found a colourful world in some of the books I didn't really know existed, and in others I found a love of animals which remains with me to this day, and in others, I found a sense of adventure usually on an individual basis to which I could not aspire. **"**

Children's Choices

It is a fact that the books which we read and enjoyed as children never truly leave us. They shaped our reading habits and character and played an important role in making us the kind of people we are today. So it is particularly satisfying to have such a wide range of titles chosen by the children themselves, as illustrated by the following choices.

Read and Enjoy!

"I would like to recommend 'Two Weeks with the Queen' by Morris Sleitzman. It tells the story of a boy whose little brother is ill with a serious disease, so he decides to write to the Queen to ask if her doctor can make his little brother well again. This is a very exciting book".

by *Daniel Watson age 10, St. Paul's Primary School*

"The book I liked was 'The House that Sailed Away' by Pat Hutchins. It tells of a terrible flood and of a house which sailed away on the flood waters. The people in the house have lots of exciting adventures as they try and control the flood. This is a really funny book".

by *Natalie Connor age 10, St. Paul's Primary School*

"The book I would recommend is 'Only You Can Save Mankind' by Terry Pratchett. This brilliant and exciting book is about a boy called Johnny who loves playing with his computer, until one day a message flashes up on his screen telling him that he is the only person who can save mankind".

by *John Pearson age 10, St. Paul's Primary School*

"I would like to recommend 'Flour Babies' by Anne Fine. It is about what happens when, as part of a science project, Simon's class are given 6 pound bags of flour and told to treat them as babies and look after them at all times.

Simon's father walked out on him and his mum when Simon was just a baby. Simon begins to realise just how hard it is to be a parent and the flour babies help him to understand why parents want the best for their children. This is a brilliant book".

by *Cheska Gillespie age 10, St. Paul's Primary School*

"My favourite book is 'James and the Giant Peach' by Roald Dahl. It is all about the marvellous adventures James has when he flies away on a giant peach. The funniest part is when the giant peach gets stuck on the Empire State Building. This is a really funny book".

by *Ashley Lennon age 9, St. Paul's Primary School*

"The book I have chosen is 'A vampire in the family' by Roy Apps. It tells what it would be like to have a real vampire in your family. The book has good colourful illustrations and is both funny and scary".

by *Danielle Devine age 11, Elder Park Primary School*

"My favourite story is 'Revolting Rhymes' by Roald Dahl. I first read this book after my teacher read a few of the poems out to the class. I like the way that Roald Dahl makes Little Red Riding Hood carry a pistol, she saves the pig's lives by killing the wicked wolf and making a handbag out of him. This is a very funny book".

by *Gordon Morrison age 11, Elder Park Primary School*

"The book I really enjoyed reading was 'Charlie and the Chocolate Factory' by Roald Dahl. It is about a boy called Charlie who wins a golden ticket in a bar of chocolate. The golden ticket means that he gets a tour round the huge chocolate factory run by the mysterious Willie Wonka. There are a lot of funny bits in this book, I really enjoyed it".

by *Lee-Anne McGarvey age 11, Elder Park Primary School*

'Flat Stanley' by Jeff Brown is my favourite book. It is about a boy called Stanley Lambchop who goes to bed one night and has a large board fall on him and flatten him. Stanley can now slide under doors instead of having to open them".

by *Scott Cooney age 10, Elder Park Primary School*

"My choice of book is called 'Teacher Trouble' by Alexander McCall Smith. It is about a girl called Jenny who moves to a new school, but because Jenny is so tall she is mistaken for the new teacher. The problem for Jenny is that she has to teach the worst class in the school. This is a funny and exciting story that you can't put down".

by *Ashley Stewart age 11, Elder Park Primary School*

"My favourite book is 'The Hiccups at No. 13 by Gyles Brandreth. This is a funny story of a boy called Hamlet Orlando Julius Caesar Brown who can't stop hiccuping. When Hamlet starts hiccuping, nobody is safe!"

by *Theresa Donnelly age 11, Elder Park Primary School*

"The book I have chosen is 'The Young Oxford Book of Ghost Stories' by Dennis Pepper. The thing I liked about this book was that, after reading it you felt that there was an unseen presence in the room with you. Spooky, eerie, creepy and scary are the words I would use to describe the best book I have ever read".

by *Laura Downie age 11, Castleton Primary School*

"My favourite book is called 'Vlad the Drac' by Ann Jungman. This is a very funny and exciting story. The funniest bit of the story is when Vlad pretends he has just eaten the postman".

by *Gordon McDermott age 11, Castleton Primary School*

"The book I would choose is 'The Return of the Mummy' by R.L. Stine. This is about a boy who goes to Egypt to visit his uncle and has a scary adventure with a 2,000 year old mummy".

by *Craig MacDonald age 10, Elder Park Primary School*

"My favourite book is 'Vlad the Drac Returns', by Ann Jungman. I liked this book because it was funny and adventurous. The character I liked best in the book was Vlad the vampire".

by *Charlotte Robertson age 9, Castleton Primary School*

"The book I really like is called 'The Secret Seven' by Enid Blyton. It is about a group of children who are always having adventures. They hold lots of meetings, so if things go wrong they always have a plan. This is a funny and adventurous story".

by *Craig Alexander Barclay age 9, Castleton Primary School*

"The book I would choose is 'The Last Battle' by C.S. Lewis. I liked this book because it was exciting and you never knew what was going to happen next. My favourite character was the King of Narnia, he was very brave and was willing to die to save his kingdom".

by *Brian McQuade age 11, Castleton Primary School*

"My favourite book is 'Casey the Utterly Impossible Horse' by Anita Feagles, it is the story of Mike who finds a horse standing at a bus stop. The strange thing is that this horse is wearing pyjamas, a yellow hat with a flower in it, a pair of sunglasses and has a balloon tied to his tail. Not only that but he can talk and he wants to live in Mike's garage. This was a really funny book".

by *Alison Docherty age 10, Saracen Primary School*

"The book I would choose is 'One Nil' by Tony Bradman. It is about a boy called Dave who loves football. When he discovers that the England football team are training at his local football ground, he comes up with a plan to miss school so that he can watch his heroes train. I would recommend this book to my friends".

by *Christopher Martin age 10, Saracen Primary School*

"The book I would choose is 'Only a Show' by Anne Fine. It is about a girl called Anna whose teacher is putting on a class show and everyone must do a 5 minute act. Anna is very nervous and does not think that she will be very good, but she surprises everyone and herself. This was a great book, I liked it a lot".

by *Christine Brewer age 9, Saracen Primary School*

Book Titles

Alcott, Louisa May – Little Women
Anderson, Hans Christian – Fairy Tales
Apps, Roy – A Vampire in the Family
Arabian Nights
Ballantyne, R.M. – Coral Island
Bestall, A.E. – Rupert the Bear stories
Blume, Judy – Are you there God? It's me, Margaret
Blyton, Enid – Adventure stories
Blyton, Enid – Famous Five stories
Blyton, Enid – Mallory Towers stories
Blyton, End – Noddy stories
Blyton, Enid – The Secret Seven
Blyton, Enid – St. Clare stories
Bradman, Tony – One Nil
Brandreth, Gyles – The Hiccups at No. 13
Brent-Dyer, Elinor M. – The Chalet School stories
Brown, Jeff – Flat Stanley
Buchan, John – The Thirty-Nine Steps
Burnett, Frances Hodgson – The Secret Garden
Carroll, Lewis – Alice in Wonderland and Through the Looking Glass
Costain, Thomas – Below the Salt
Crompton, Richmal – Just William
Crompton, Richmal – William's Crowded Hours
Dahl, Roald – Charlie and the Chocolate Factory
Dahl, Roald – James and the Giant Peach
Dahl, Roald – Revolting Rhymes
Derwent, Lavinia – The Adventures of Tammy Troot
Dickens, Charles – Oliver Twist
Dickens, Charles – A Tale of Two Cities
Doyle, Arthur Conan – White Company
Falkner, John – Moonfleet
Feagles, Anita – Casey the Utterly Impossible Horse
Fine, Anne – Flour Babies
Fine, Anne – Only a Show
Forester, C.S. – Hornblower stories
Golding, William – Lord of the Flies
Goscinny & Uderzo – Asterix stories
Grahame, Kenneth – The Wind in the Willows
Green, Roger Lancelyn – The Adventures of Robin Hood
Green, Roger Lancelyn – King Arthur and his Knights of the Round Table
Grimm's Fairy Tales
Hergé – Tintin stories
Holling, Holling Clancy – The Tree in the Trail

Holm, Anne – I am David
Hughes, Thomas – Tom Brown's School Days
Hutchins, Pat – The House that Sailed Away
Jansson, Tove – The Moomintroll stories
Johns, Captain F.W. – Biggles
Jungman, Ann – Vlad the Drac
Jungman, Ann – Vlad the Drac Returns
Kantor, MacKinlay – Andersonville
Kingsley, Charles – The Heroes
Kipling, Rudyard – just so Stories
Kipling, Rudyard – Kim
Lang, Andrew – Fairy Tales series
Lewis, C.S. – The Last Battle
Lewis, C.S. – The Lion, the Witch and the Wardrobe
Lindgren, Astrid – Pippi Longstocking
London, Jack – White Fang
McLean, Allan Campbell – The Hill of the Red Fox
Marryat, Captain – Masterman Ready
Mitchell, Evelyn – The Palomino Pony
Pepper, Dennis – The Young Oxford Book of Ghost Stories
Pratchett, Terry – Only You Can Save Mankind
Ransome, Arthur – Swallowdale
Ransome, Arthur – Swallows and Amazons
Richards, Frank – Greyfriars stories (Billy Bunter)
Salinger, J.D. – The Catcher in the Rye
Seuss, Dr. – The Cat in the Hat
Sewell, Anna – Black Beauty
Sleitzman, Morris – Two Weeks with the Queen
Smith, Alexander McCall – Teacher Trouble
Stevenson, Robert Louis – The Child's Garden of Verses
Stevenson, Robert Louis – Kidnapped
Stevenson, Robert Louis – Treasure Island
Stewart, Mary – The Moonspinners
Stine, R.L. – The Return of the Mummy
Swift, Jonathan – Gulliver's Travels
Thomas, Dylan – Under Milk Wood
Tolkien, J.R. – The Hobbit
Tolkien, J.R. – Lord of the Rings
Trease, Geoffrey – Bows Against the Barons
Tritten, Charles – Heidi Grows Up
Twain, Mark – Tom Sawyer
Uttley, Alison – Little Grey Rabbit stories
Verne, Jules – 20,000 Leagues Under the Sea
Weiss, J.R. – Swiss Family Robinson
Williamson, Henry – Tarka the Otter